PATRICK HAMILTON

A TRAGEDY

OF

THE REFORMATION IN SCOTLAND, 1528

BY

T. P. JOHNSTON

" *The old order changeth* "

WILLIAM BLACKWOOD AND SONS
EDINBURGH AND LONDON
MDCCCLXXXII

NOTE.

THE aim of the author has been, in the first
place, to present an accurate historical pic-
ture of the times described, and of the interesting
and earnest young life for whom they were, alas!
too much "out of joint;" and, in the next, to illus-
trate the nature of the "disastrous feud" between
old and new in matters of faith which, in the
sixteenth century, had an outburst of more than
usual fury—a feud which is of old standing, and
constantly liable to renewal.

CARNBEE, *November* 1881.

PATRICK HAMILTON.

PATRICK HAMILTON was the first to fall a martyr
at the commencement in earnest of that struggle
which ended in the Reformation. His is the first
name remembered by Knox in his history of that
event. It is also the first inscribed upon the obelisk
which stands by St Andrews Bay, commemorating
five brave men who, in those years and in that
city, "perished by fire" for their adhesion to Protestant principles.

He had the advantage of an ancestry both noble
and gifted. His father, Sir Patrick Hamilton of
Kincavel, was a knight so famous that his exploits

have been celebrated by no less than three chroni-
clers of as many countries; and his mother, Cath-
erine Stewart, was a grand-daughter of our Scotch
King James II.

When only a boy, but already, according to the
easy fashion of the time, Abbot of Ferne, he went
abroad to study at Louvain, and likewise at Paris,
where Scotchmen then possessed a college of their
own, founded with their own money, about the time
of Robert the Bruce. In 1523, when eighteen
years of age, he came home a Master of Arts,
to enter the University of St Andrews, and to take
up his residence in that centre of Scotland's ecclesi-
astical life. What kind of man he was, we learn
chiefly from his friend and fellow-canon Alexander
Alane, who loved him and cherished his memory,
and frequently takes occasion to speak of him in
the course of his expository works. In character

he was honest and earnest. Although an abbot, he loathed the gown and cowl that covered so many a lewd hypocrite of a monk, and refused to wear them. He was learned, the New Testament and Plato being his chief reading. His cherished copy of the Gospels he yielded on his way to the stake into the hands of a friend. He was a true Christian in spirit. "We have a good and gentle Lord," were his own words; "let us follow His steps." He was a man of taste and culture, music being the art in which he excelled; and we have the interesting fact recorded, that on one occasion the Cathedral Church of St Andrews echoed to a choral service of which he was the composer, and which he himself conducted in the capacity of precentor.

It is on the day of the performance of this piece that the tragedy is made to open.

CHIEF PERSONS REPRESENTED.

PATRICK HAMILTON, Abbot of Ferne.

JAMES BEATON, Archbishop of St Andrews.

PRIOR CAMPBELL.

JOHN ANDREW DUNCAN, a Wickliffite.

RALPH, his servant.

ISOBEL, a lady of rank, afterwards wife to Hamilton.

KATHERINE, Hamilton's sister.

CITIZENS, STUDENTS, &c.

The scene is principally laid in St Andrews.

PATRICK HAMILTON.

ACT I.

SCENE I.

St Andrews—the Cathedral. Citizens issuing after service.

1st Citizen. A stately service, and its ornament
This choral piece of the young Hamilton,
"*Praise Him all angels !*"   When the voices rose
In one great host—basses, ecstatic trebles,
And all the kindred company of sounds
Filling the church, and echoing round the roof
A thousandfold—I thought that angels' selves
Joined hallelujahs.   For my own part now

I like this *figured song*, which comes in vogue
More than the *plain chant* of St Gregory.

   2d Cit. In sacred things I love no novelty;
Leave me the olden and habitual.

   1st Cit. Ever I make the new and better welcome.
Religion would I have a cup for thirst,
Not a mere ancient vase—a curio.

   2d Cit. I stand in the old paths.

   1st Cit.   Tempt but my feet
With any new that promise fairer fields,
And I will tread them gaily without fear.
Not yet I think we've reached the utmost bounds
Of Truth's bright realm, nor will the next step
       plunge us
In error's poisoned waste.   But tell me, now,
What stranger preached the sermon?

   2d Cit.   Prior John
     of Pittenweem.

1st Cit.   What ! do the priors turn friars
And climb our pulpits?   Then we'll hack the post
With a deep notch to-day to mark a wonder.

    2d Cit. Yet he spoke well.

    1st Cit.   Well ! sapless chaff his
        doctrine.

When one has read what says the Apostle John,
One sifts the nonsense talked by John the prior ;
And his tirade against the Lutherans
Had more of rage than argument.   Not much
I like this sudden stir of our chief priests.
When thus the " dumb dogs " bark, I have a fear
Their bite comes next.

                    But here our roads divide.
Farewell !   [*Exit.*

    2d Cit. Farewell !   Infected too with heresy ;
Amazing how the Lutherish fever spreads !
It simmers in the blood of half one meets.   [*Exit.*

ARCHBISHOP BEATON *and* PRIOR JOHN *issuing.*

Arch. B. A powerful sermon, prior! take my
    thanks—
One suited to the times.   Men must be told
What errors are abroad, and told by those
Whose words have weight.   Too long these preach-
    ing friars,
Who rant of Mary and of miracles,
Paint Purgatory's pangs with such fine zest,
And preach the horse-leech daughter's gospel, "Give!"
Too long these cushion-thumping mountebanks
Have had the pulpit to themselves ; 'tis we
Must mount it now, display our rhetoric,
Catch the misguided public by the ears,
And steer it right, if we would save the Church.
I tell you, Prior, times are critical.
I have some friends abroad who send me news,

And half of Germany, they say, is lost—

Lost to the Pope's dominion and the faith.

Here in St Andrews, spite of the new Act,

The books of Luther and Erasmus swarm.

Last night I caught my servant in his bed

Reading the Tyndale Gospel by his lamp :

I cuffed the fellow's ears, and flung the book

At once into the fire.   That's but a sample.

Go through this town by night, and where you see

A window with a gleam within that burns

To meet the dawn, know that beside it sits

Some Bible-reader.   Nothing but Bible now.

There's not a canon in St Leonard's there

But hides the guilty volume in his sleeve,

And steals a glance when he should con his office.

That hive's a-hum with heresy.   Oh yes,

I know the goings-on within these walls ;

My little birds bring news.

This Hamilton,
Whose tuneful handiwork you just have heard,
The choral piece was his.   How liked you it ?
    Prior J. Never ask me; I have as little ear
As any cuckoo.   Music's a mere toy.
        Arch. B. He led the choir too.   Yes, the lad has
        skill—
Has old Sir Patrick's talent, not a doubt ;
Most like he has his obstinacy too,
And fiery spirit—for you know the proverb,
Like sire, like colt.
                Well I recall the day—
A black one too for me—seven years ago,
When th' old knight died on Edinburgh street.
Some taunt of cowardice made hot his blood ;
Away he burst, thrashed down the spears like straws,
And died at length, one man o'erborne by hundreds.
I saw him in this son of his to-day :

The same brave brow, a face sincere and calm,
Lifted upon you like a night with stars—
The same firm hand, although it held no sword;
But tense and earnest kept the choir in time.
I marked his eye if any voice rose flat—
It flashed as I have seen the father's flash.
This stripling troubles me. He heads a set
Of youths that read the Scriptures in their Greek,
And kindle over Plato, and conceive
They sit at Truth's own source, and need no help
Of the Church rope and wheel to draw it for them;
Have been to foreign universities,
And learned the newest modes in heresy;
Returning home, find all things out of joint—
Ourselves, the clergy, dullards, worldly men,
Wanting the Pauline fervour, and our lives
Short of their high ideal; so they talk
Their mind about, encouraging discontent,

And evermore they cause the cry grow louder
For reformation.   Hamilton leads this,
And more than once I would have dealt with him,
But the lad's friends stand high.   His pale face, too,
Looks resolute ; breeding, mark, does not bend
Like slave that has the " yes, sir " in his blood ;
And after all, perhaps, Gamaliel's way
May be more prudent.

    Prior J.   Not my mind at all.
I never thought Gamaliel's counsel sound ;
'Twas plausible, but wholly ruinous.
So found the Sanhedrim when all was done.
When all Jerusalem was upside down,
Religious revolution in full blaze,
Past all their power to quench,—when that time came,
I warrant that the angry beards went wag—
Fists in his face—and loud the rabbis scolded,
Cursing themselves and him for simple fools.

No, no, Archbishop, act ! let not things slide.

For instance, now, if Samson's foxes ran

Among your corn, a firebrand at each tail,

Would not you seize the vermin, quench the fire ?

God's wounds, I'd bend him ! I've no sympathy

With those young fools who think that their first
    squeal

Was wisdom's earliest voice. Reform the Church !

Is it not now on all sides prosperous ?—

New buildings rising, a great work at Crail,

Glasgow, and Biggar, money pouring in,

New zeal upspringing, and a stricter duty.

Daily our churches now are open for service—

A lovely custom. Oh, but, by the way,

Tell me of Hepburn here, your worthy prior.

Reigns his sultana still within the walls ?

   Arch. B. Gone !

   Prior J. So your mandate drove her into exile ?

B

Arch. B. Not very quickly.

Prior J.   Ha, the daring rogue!

He stood out for the fair one with some spirit ;

But in the very Abbey ! You were right ;

It was not to be thought of. Ah, the old story !

　　　C'est l'amour, l'amour,

　　　Qui fait le monde à la ronde.

We are not angels, either you or I,

But Hepburn goes too far, the rogue, too far.

I heard some tales of him to make you laugh :

Some day an irate spouse will offer him

A victim to Dame Venus.

　　　　　　　Phew ! the east wind

Blows keenly on these naked cliffs of yours ;

I hope your claret sits in the smile of the fire ;

Preaching is thirsty work, and hungry too,—

It melts the flesh from off a portly man

To sweat in a pulpit. But I'll make up loss

With your good cheer, Archbishop; well I know
What can your cook. There should be wild-duck now
On those sea-flats. No better dish than teal
Roasted with chestnuts, or a widgeon larded
And stewed with oysters. Did not I rise winner
Last time we played? I think some crowns of yours
Went jingling gaily homeward in my pouch.

    Arch. B. You smote me hard.

    Prior J.   Take your revenge
       to-night;
Let the dice rattle to a goodly tune—
Deep stakes for me that stir the mettle up,
And set the heart a-thumping like a soldier's
When death or fortune stand upon the chance
Of half a minute.

                So I say again
The Church does well enough, could we but stay
This German plague. I hate that rascal land;

It reeks with all malaria.   The black death
Came to us thence, I think.

    Arch. B.   I have a letter
Writ from my nephew David at Arbroath.
He is most earnest for some instant steps
Against the heretics.

    Prior. J.   Take his advice.
A strong man he—no puling, praying monk.
If I know men, the world will hear of him ;
He will be cardinal yet.

    Arch. B.   'Tis entering in,
And having to go forward.

    Prior J.   Forward go,
A sniff of burning flesh might clear the air.

    Arch. B. Hold, hold, Prior !   Nay, not that—you
        make me shudder !—
But something of a warning or a threat
Might serve the turn.   I am most loath to move ;

I fear the result. I am most loath to move ;
But whatsoever blow we fix to strike,
Upon young Hamilton that blow must fall.

[*Exeunt.*

PATRICK HAMILTON, *issuing from a side-door
toward the sea.*

Ham. At length 'tis over, ending as all ends.
Th' ideal flies us, a 'scaped butterfly,
Achievement stays, the maimed one in our hand.
Now to the sea-beach, and beside the sea—
Oh sweet and very dear to me the sea !
Sometimes far inland in the sultry heat
So have I longed for it, I laid me down
'Neath leaves a-rustling, there to dream and think ;
I felt the freshness in my soul of waves—
Great ocean, all-embracing, sweetening all !
It visits every shore with equal love,

Like the great God's, and clasps the islands round.

It links me to the brotherhood of men ;

That water lapped but late on Afric's coast.

A thousand tokens at my feet it lays

From lands far distant—here a palm-leaf lies,

And there a Havre fisherman's cork float.

Out of its mighty multitudinous sound,

Like hallelujahs of the praising world

In John's Apocalypse, chorals I shape—

Resolve the din into articulate score,

As sculptors in a rude mass pile the clay,

Then seize it in their hands and fashion it.

Music of all arts surely highest stands ;

But why on any art will men look cold,

Or why will they disuse a single power

Gifted by God to the rich human soul?

Still prone to be one-sided is mankind,

Like birds, that if they strongly run on land,

Or swim on sea, or dive, have dwindled wings,

Bearing them no more to high realms of air.

There's Roger now, the best voice in the choir,

Sings like a man inspired, yet, Mass once o'er,

Runs to his revel and profanity.

And that new painter working in the church,

Beneath whose hand the roof grows to a heaven

Shining with angels and the eyes of saints,

They lash him daily to his scaffolding,

Lest drunken from that height he fall below

. And dash in pieces.   Brother Mark, again,

Pious and good, a conscientious soul,

Screens his cell window lest the sun shine in

Too warm and beautiful, and stops his ears

If he but hear a strain that's gaily pitched.

" Love not the world ! " he groans—" love not the
　　world ! "

I would not thus be maimed of half my mind,

But to the height and pinnacle of my being
I would be man complete, as nature meant me.

> Perfect us, Lord,
> The work of Thy hand,
> So may we stand
> Before Thee approving.

> All that Thou givest us
> Gladly enjoying,
> Richly employing
> All powers in us moving.

> Mind for all knowledge,
> Heart for all love,
> While still above
> Faith's anchor is holding.

Eye for all beauty,

Ear for all sweetness,

Thus to completeness

Our life, Lord, unfolding.

Prince 'mid our powers must ever Faith preside,

The rest his friends and sweet companions.

Faith is the Apollo's voice that calls the Nine

To ply in concert all their heavenly tasks.

Man lives by Faith.

Yes, and a Church too lives

Only by faith. See here this empty shell

I trundle with my foot upon the sand,

How art-rich and how perfected a work !

Buttressed, built up, and carved and pinnacled.

Here's architecture, painting,—to my ear,

Yes, music too,—why then does it lie here

With useless things, with withering sea-weed,

Thin skeletons, and bleaching scraps of wreck
Cast out by the great sea?   No life within ;
The subtle spirit that first created this,
Kept it and used, is gone.   It is a church
Where faith has ceased to be—a church that lies
Slow rotting on the shore of moving time.

Now to yon cove by the high cliffs enscreened,
There on the sun-warmed sand to lie and read.
What might that look mean which to-day in church
Twice the Archbishop fixed upon my face?
Twice as I turned I saw his eye withdraw
With a quick glitter, like a sword to its sheath.
It was a strange look, and it jarred me so,
I almost missed the bar and beat false time.

Castle of St Andrews

Enter PRIOR CAMPBELL.

Campbell. Musing, my friend?

Ham. Ah, Campbell, glad

to meet.

How went my choral?

Cam. Excellent, time and tone.

Ham. A little more rehearsal had been well.

How bright the day, how fresh the smell of the sea—

To our old nook together 'mong the rocks.

· How sweet is life with nature, friendship, art,

And the great thoughts that live for us in books!

Sad, did death call us but to black despair—

To say farewell to earth, and sea, and sky,

And dear familiar faces that we love;

No gleam of light beyond, nor any hope

Of a new heaven to come and a new earth.

Ye shining planets, that we ne'er should know

Our brothers in you dwelling—never look
With nearer eyes upon the heart of things.
Still must I think that we shall know more yet,
And see more ; that life moves to some great end—
Fulfilment, not frustration, is its goal,—
Children of God, heirs of immortal life,
As our great Master taught the world to think.
I hold that true, Campbell ; I hold that true.

[Exeunt.

SCENE II.

*St Andrews, near the Castle.   Officers with Dutch
Skipper in charge, rabble following.*

Crowd. Into the castle with the Lutheran !
Beneath the sea-tower he will have to buzz
Like blue-fly in a bottle.

[Exeunt officers and part of crowd.

Student. Friend, what's this?

2d Stud. Purity of the faith. Heard you no noise
Of trumpets at the cross an hour ago?
Our Parliament has issued a new Edict,
And through the length of the land the sheriffs blare it.
All books of Luther and the heretics
Are strictly interdict; none may import them,
Nor even read them, nor debate of them,
Save only learned clerks in colleges,
And even then with no approval, mark you—
Only with fore intent of damning them.

   1st Stud. Call that debate? Why, 'tis a puppet-
      fight,
Always the same puppet knocked upon the head.

   Man from the crowd. What mutter you? Mean
      you to mock the Edict?

   1st Stud. Hold 'off, you drunkard! Whither do
      you thrust?

Man. Thrust! I would thrust this knife in
 through the ribs

Of every hell-fire heretic—'od's blood!

If you be one—you look a candle-burner

Over your books, you tallow-face.

 1st Stud.   Put up

That whittle, brave defender of the faith!

Keep it to pare your bend and cordovan.

Go home and grunt over your lingels, man;

You will do mischief staggering thus about.

Ne sutor ultra crepidam.

 Man.   What, Latin!

Mark you the Edict, we'll no heresy.

Scotland, the Edict says, has still been clean

From filth of that kind, and we'll keep it clean.

Confound your Bibles, say I, and your Greek.

 Man's Wife. Give him no heed, my sweet young
  gentleman,

Some venomous ale has jumbled his poor head :

He's always theological when drunk ;

But oh, I hope here is no heresy.

Ugh ! how the very name just makes me grue !

What do they tell me ?   Luther's coming now

Over the North Sea on a magic cloak

From Satan's loom—it tames the sea to oil—

And spell-books carries he beneath his arm ;

That when he comes he'll strike the land with plagues

Worse than old Egypt's—fire, and hail, and lice.

Some sailors passed him three days out at sea :

They crossed themselves, and cried out, " Satan,
     hence ! "

When with great thunderclaps and fire he vanished.

I have all this from a good holy man

That comes our way at each half-year or so,

To hear confession and give absolution.

   Man. Rascal, he comes too often—gets my money.

You hoard for him, though I should eat dry loaf,
And I must cobble his shoes or give him new ones.
You and he are too friendly.

   Man's Wife.   Hush, you fool !
Home to your lapstone, or I'll clout your ears.

                           [*Exeunt.*

   1*st Stud.* This is a sample now of the sage public,—
Mere hollow instruments for others' breath
To blow through, and their stops, which crafty hands
Know how to manage and to sound in turn—
A range of prejudices, nothing more.
How would these folks yell now at an *auto da fe,*
Or wreck an abbey !   But I wait to hear
More of the skipper who just passed in charge.

   2*d Stud.* He sails a little craft 'twixt this and
        Holland,
With pots and cordovan and woollen stuffs,
Fabrics of the far East, and suchlike goods.

This morning with the tide he put in here,

But scarce his rope's fixed when they jump aboard

And turn his bales out—all heart heretics—

Packed full of Bibles and High German tracts;

Good market is there for such contraband,

And tempting profits in St Andrews now.

Such litter spread the quay! velvets, furs, silks,

The rarest ivories, wealth of silver cups.

Guess you where such things go? Why, most of them

Up to the castle yonder, or elsewhere,

To deck our churchmen's pretty ladies out,

And grace their dainty boudoirs. But the books,

The fresh white sheets, grievous to see them piled

Upon the pier, and without pity burned,

Writhing and twisting up as if in pain.

I snatched a prize, though, while the mass was blazing:

See here, beneath my cloak—'tis a *bonne bouche*,

Curled like autumnal leaves, and badly browned,

C

But legible enough were I once home.

 1*st Stud. Erasmi colloq*——

 2*d Stud.*   Hush ! yon ugly rogue,

Who leans upon his staff and pricks his ear,

May be a spy of Beaton's. Let us hence.

            [*Exeunt.*

SCENE III.

Airdrie, in the east of Fife. The house of JOHN
  DUNCAN [1]—*present,* DUNCAN, PATRICK HAMIL-
  TON, GILBERT WINRAM, *&c.;* RALPH, *an old*
  retainer, odd and privileged.

 Duncan. Ralph, clear the tables. There's a slice
   yet left

Of that good haunch. He was a lusty buck,

      [1] See Note A, p. 107.

And gave us a long run. Game now grows scarce
On the Kingsmuir. That heron we set up
Below Pitarthie, fat was he and gorged,
Else had we lost him, for my hawks' new bells
Are over-heavy. Here, hawk, catch! Well done!
Oh, but cease screaming. Come, dogs ; bones, dogs,
 bones!
Fill up the wine-jugs, Ralph. Broach the big butt
That Frenchman sent us whom we saved and lodged
Two years since, when his ship and crew were lost
On the Carr rock. " *Tu es mon père,*" he'd pipe,
" *Sauveur !* " and thank me twenty times a-day.
Yet, rogue, he would have stolen my wife to France—
Would he not, wife? Nay, no protesting now.
'Twas wheedle, wheedle, bowing, scraping, dying,
" Heart at your feet, Madame."

  Mrs Duncan.   Your old joke, John.
He only said I was a mother to him,

And told me all his troubles, and would weep,
Speaking of his own mother.

  Dun.   Ah, his mother!
Always *ma mère* with monsieur. Oh, I know,
There is a sort of men—and the French land
Breeds them the most—must still be burrowing
Into the soft heart of some womankind;
It is their pastime.

  Mrs Dun.   John, you just were jealous.

  Dun. Nay, hardly that, goodwife, else had I soon
Put him where first I found him—in the sea.
Howe'er, I'll warrant that the grateful soul
Sent us no meagre juice of his land's grape.
It should be ripe by this. *Ah, pays de France!*
Here is your gay soul and your summer sun.
Drive the Fife fog out of our colder clay!
Empty the flagon, friends. Would Beaton, now,
Not smack his lips o'er this? eh, Hamilton?

This is true "vinum theologicum."

Winram is Rechabite, he loves the spring.

 Winram. Thus does it stand with me. I am like
  one

Who sees a murder, and from that time forth

Hates gleam of steel. But for the vice of drink,

Our monks had clearer brains and cleaner lives.

 Dun. True ; turn them all adrift, the lousy crew.

"Good people, come and kiss the dear saint's bone.

Come, buy a pardon cheap." Bah ! my blood boils

To think how they befool the simple folk.

Turn them adrift, I say, and give us men

To think and speak some guidance.

 Win.   Scarce are such.

Thinking is rarer far than repetition.

One man invents a tune, and then a host

Grind it on a hand-organ.

 Dun.   True again.

Nay, we'll not ask for prophets and wise men,

They are at all times but a scanty breed ;

But at the least let us have men to read

The Word of God, and tell what therein stands,

Making John speak to us, and Paul, and Christ.

Let them dip down their cups into the fount,

And give truth's water to a dying people.

    Win. Heard you of Meldrum's death-scene ?

    Dun.   Not a word.

    Win. Oh, it was all the talk, and to my mind

It was a scandal to religion's name.

He had some sudden quarrel over cards

With a hot soldier new from the French wars,

So out they went and fought upon the Scores.

The swords had barely flashed when he was down,

Blood oozing from his mouth, his breast dug through.

They bore him to a tavern, then sent

For priest to shrive him, for his time seemed short.

There came not one, but a whole flock of crows,
Both black and grey.   From every side the friars,
Tucking their gowns for haste, came running down.
An hour they fought above the dying man
Who should confess him, clamouring at each ear.
His sin and its forgiveness troubled him;
But, as it chanced, a monk had in his pouch
A pardon of the Pope's—had come too late
For its right owner.   They erased his name
And wrote in Meldrum's, and the thing was done.
Then came the will to make.   They shared the spoil,
Bequeathed his means for masses to their houses,
Then seized his torpid hand and made him sign.
" His widow," say you? *Corban,* 'tis a gift;
She and the children may receive their share
In rations in some convent, so 'tis fixed.
And then they laid him out upon the floor,
Sprinkled with ashes—thus St Francis died,

It seems—and over him a grey monk's coat,

Upon his head a cowl, and in each hand

A lighted taper.   Then through all the house

Rose such a sound of chanting and of prayers,

A *hummil-bummil* of quite unknown tongues—

A perfect Babel till the man was dead.

　　Dun. In pace, Domine, dimittas me !

Rather than to be pestered thus and robbed

In my last hour, I had made end on Flodden—

Face to the stars had given my soul to God.

　　Enter RALPH, *who whispers to* HAMILTON.

　　Ralph. Would you please start ? the mules are at

　　　　the door

This good half-hour, and the valises on.

　　Dun. What say you, Ralph ? There was small life

　　　　to spare

Next morning when you found me on the grass,

Stiff with the hoar-frost? 'Twas you saved me, Ralph,
Else soon death's frost had gripped me by the heart.

Ralph. Ay, ay, folk give their friends a deal of
toil
Running and fighting where they have no call.

Dun. For king and country, sir.

Ralph.   Ay, that's the word;
But just another time I'll bide at Airdrie—
Soft bed, good meat, and smaller chance of blows.

Dun. You love not soldiering, Ralph.

Ralph.   Not much, I grant—
It's mere rash folly; yet there's one kind worse,
That folk should fash themselves about some thing,
What is it called?—the truth, the cause, so on,
And heat their blood about it, make a stir,
And get their lives in peril. Well-a-wat,
I may be mad, as oft enough I'm told,
But such rank madness ne'er was in my skull.

Dun. A man must do his duty, Ralph.

Ralph.   Awell,

There must be different natures, I just think.

I see the barn-door cock goes douce about

Among his hens, and cackles o'er a pickle ;

The game-cock jumps for ever on the dikes,

And claps his wings and crows, and scorns the world.

Quick nerve, keen eye, he looks about and runs,

Daring and doing, ruling the whole yard,—

Just so I think there are two kinds of men ;

And I am barn-door sort, I love my ease.

Dun. A glass of ale for Ralph. Stop man ! so fast !

Where are your manners? have you not a health ?

Shame not my house as if you drank for thirst.

RALPH.

Gentles, I pledge you the birdie that flees

From the gled and his claws to a bield o'er the seas ;

Pledge you the laddie that's leaving his home,
Seeking a kinder land o'er the salt foam.

I know a bonnie boat rocking to-night
Down by Crail shore in the summer moonlight.

Wings of a dove are its sails flapping free,
Waiting to waft him out o'er the wide sea.

Lord, be his refuge wherever he dwell—
This to his health, and a loving farewell.

     (*Turning to* HAMILTON *and drinking.*)

 Dun. What's this? What mean you, Ralph? and
  Hamilton,
Why look you thus? and all the night you've sat
With something in your face—what means it all?

 Ham. Ralph speaks the truth, and lets a secret out
I feared to tell, but must have told at length.

To-night I leave you ; if you ask me why,
Read that and learn.

     (*Throwing a paper upon the table.*)

 Dun. (*reading it.*) Great heavens ! a summons here
From the Archbishop Beaton to attend
And answer to a charge of heresy !

 All. Summoned for heresy !

 Ham.   The bolt has fallen.
Long time this thunder-cloud has brooded dark
Above my head.   I knew the time would come ;
In the Archbishop's face to-day I read
That it was near.   Some little time I walked
Upon the beach, and when I reached my home
This paper waited me.   My plans are laid.
A friendly skipper takes me hence to-night
In his small craft to Holland.   I would see
The master Luther, hear his very voice,
Receive his counsel.   Well I know how men

Will call me coward. Beaton too will sneer.

I've strength to bear all this a while. God knows

My father's son's no coward. If I go,

'Tis not to hide, to live in craven ease,

To eat and drink secure. I go to don

My plate of mail, to close the rivets up,

To prove my sword and spear, and brace my arm—

Then for the joust *à l'outrance.* Nay, I go

To ask, " My father, is the cup thine own? "

To pray and to bethink me. Time will show.

Meanwhile, my friends, judge kindly, trust me, wait.

    Dun. Curse the proud priest! He dare not do

      thee harm.

Stay! face him! I will arm a force of men,

Surround the council-chamber where they sit,

And dare them even frown. Earl Arran's nephew,

Son of a king's granddaughter, they were bold

To touch a hair of thee!

Ham.   Dear friend, 'tis fixed,

Winram and John here bear me company;

Even now the boat awaits us at Crail quay.

    Ralph. Would you please start? the night wear

        fast away—

I doubt if now the moon will light us down—

And by this time the skipper's dancing wild;

The tide's an hour on ebb and the wind fair.

    Dun. Well, if it must be; but this is mos

        sudden.

To the boat's side we all will bring you down,

And there take our farewell.   [*Exeunt*

SCENE IV.

On board ship in mid-ocean. HAMILTON *on deck alone.*

Ham. Softly the sea-bird is floating
　　On the smooth ocean's breast,
　Round is the sea-mist shining,
　　And over all is rest.

　Never a sound but the ripple
　　That runs at the vessel's side—
　Only a passing whisper
　　That comes from the stranger tide.

　Never a breath comes hither
　　To tell of the stir on the shore ;
　Gone are the voices and passions,
　　Gone is the city's roar.

Gone the whole loud land shaking,
   With life in its valleys and plains,—
Sunk 'neath the distant horizon,
   And only its memory remains.

'Tis as I'd died—and had floated
   Far from the world of life,
Into the silent region,
   Out of the din and the strife.

Gone my keen zest for things human,
   Heat both of longing and hate—
Calmness impartial succeeding
   Where passion was late.

Yonder my mortal image
   Moves on the far shore of time—
Ah, self! with an infinite pity
   I look from this rest sublime,—

See thee amidst thy striving,
  Throbbing of heart and toil,
Wandering and seeking and falling,
  Poor stranger on earth's strange soil!

Yonder my mortal being
  Standeth completed and done—
What was there worth the doing
  These days underneath the sun?

What was there worth the doing?
  The right alone and the true :
The right—that I did it, I did it;
  The truth—that I spoke as I knew.

Ah, there is nought to suffice us
  But this, as we leave earth's sod,
Floating out into the silence,
  Alone with conscience and God!

D

'Tis Sabbath now in Scotland, my dear land,
Though wild and rude and hardly kind to me;
Dear for my own forefathers and their graves,
Dear for the men still living on thy hills—
Fain would I serve thee, if I only might;
Not fighting for thy sake 'gainst angry foes,
For I am but a clerk and not a knight.
Mine is the voice, not sword; yet in my task
Of peace I would be faithful as a knight,
Telling thee all the truth as wise men know it,
Hiding no jot for fear, and pushing still,
Dear land, thy day of light and beauty on.
'Tis Sabbath now: o'er all the peaceful scene
The people gather to the house of prayer—
Old men and young, fair women, children sweet.
By hawthorn hedges and by springing corn
I hear their voices warble as they pass.
These seek their meat from God. Oh, thinker thou,

O priest, O Christ-sent, feed God's people well
With thy best truth; fail not for sloth or dread,
Else art thou traitor to thy land and them.

Enter CAPTAIN, *Sailors following.*

Captain. Good sir, I have come hither with the
    crew,
Begging a kindness. We are simple men,
And have but little knowledge of God's lore;
Our lives are spent at sea; we never hear
The sweet church-bells or sound of preacher's voice.
One day flows like another overhead,
While we must watch the wind and work the
    ship;
And yet we see God's wonders in the deep,
And fear His name. A sailor may be rough,
But has his own thoughts on the deck at night,

When earth's great ship sails through the lights of
      heaven.
You are a clerk, sir, and, I hear them say,
Have this new knowledge that has long lain hid,
But now comes up to bless the souls of men.
Somewhat thereof we've heard, and would hear more;
It seems to us the way of God in truth.
If you would please to speak, we're free to listen.
The ship moves with the tide, needing no care,
And 'twill be eve ere Flushing comes in sight.

   Ham. Fain would I see the day when every man
Might for himself the words of Jesus read,
And when the great Evangel, written plain
In the same tongue his mother taught him, lay
In every cottage and in each sea-chest.
Oh, but the Christ spake plain to simple men;
He told the Father's love who gives them life,
Feeds, guides, and pardons, and, best gift of all,

Sent His own precious Son to tell them this—

To speak it, live it, yes, and die it too.

Oh then, receive it ; think not to win heaven

By painful penances with heart stone-cold,

But trust God ; be His friend as He is yours ;

Be sure His love shone earlier than the sun,

And still will shine when sun and moon are dark.

FAITH is the root within from which outsprings,

First CHARITY, the virtue of all acts,

For he alone that Father has in heaven,

Has brothers and has sisters on the earth ;

Then HOPE, that makes the greatness of our life,

Breaks down the tomb's dark wall, and opens out

Reaches of far perspective to our sight.

As in a glowing sunset on the sea

Looms a new country slowly rising up,

With strange white towers and glittering window-
    lights,

While every heart with expectation beats
As the ship nears it over shining waves,—
So to HOPE's vision shines the better land,
End of Life's voyage and our spirit's home.
Take my last word : Christ is a gentle Lord,
Whom all the world should bless and magnify ;
Him let us follow.

    (*Sailor's voice.*)   Land ho ! Land ahead ![1]

[1] See Note B, p. 109.

Marburg an der Lahn

ACT II.

SCENE I.

A Wood near a Mansion.

Isobel. The Morn has leapt into the wood
    Across the dewy miles,
  And chases night with spears of light
    Throughout the arching aisles,

  The golden reeds divide the gloom,
    And where a shaft may hit
  The mossy stems of molten gems,
    Down drips a rivulet.

Laughing she flies; her odorous breath
    Fills all the leafy bowers;
Her dewy feet sip kisses sweet
    From lips of waking flowers.

Night flies, with all her blinded brood
    Within her arms lying,
And timid things on muffled wings
    In her cold shadow flying;—

Far down by many an ivied shade
    And many a noisome hollow,
To deepest dells where safe she dwells,
    And morning may not follow.

Sing high upon a gilded spray,
    O linnet burning bright!

Dance humming things on gauzy wings
Amid this blissful light !

And fill from mossy floor to roof
The greenwood's pillared hall,
With one full sound from all things round,
Glad nature's matinal !

I cannot rest abed, but must be up
Soon as the long sweet sunbeams light the dew.
Six weary months since my love crossed the sea,
Six weary months I've wandered here alone,
Finding all places empty where we strayed
So oft together—living on memories :
How here we sat, how here we gathered flowers,
Or searched for purple berries in the heath ;
Here held long sweet discourse of earnest things,
Walking belated till the risen moon

Had barred our path with shadows of great stems,
Silvered the leaves around and rippling brooks,
Shone on our cheeks, and changed this common
    world
To some new sphere enchanted, marvellous,
Where nothing was but beauty, thought, and love,
And we two moved alone there all in all.

Enter KATHERINE.

Katherine. What is between my palms?

Iso.   Show me.

Kath.   Nay,
    guess.

Iso. Unclasp, unclasp; I see it peep—a letter,
And I am sure from him. (*Reads.*) He comes, Kate,
    comes,
And soon, for this has lingered on the way.
Here are his own dear words: he hopes, he says,

Before the ripened apples shall have dropt,

Before the scarlet flush has left the woods,

Before November winds have swept the flowers,

Once more to sit in the old garden-seat.

. And——but, dear Kate, the rest is all my own——

Oh sweet remembrances and sweeter hopes !

My day was dark, Kate, but is shining up

In a great glory of tumultuous light.

Oh smile not to behold my whirl of joy ;

You know not what it is to wait and wait

For that once presence makes the world not blank—

To sicken through the sultry summer heat,

Loathing the flowers, the birds, the sighing wind ;

And all the night to lie in trickling tears,

Picturing sad scenes of death and deathless vows,

Last kisses, parting tokens, long farewells.

Dear Kate, you know not what it is to love

As I your brother ; we have grown to one :

I live but in his life, see with his eyes—

Beauty, religion, all things, what they are

Revealed themselves to me alone in him,

Light of my world; and I cannot look

On any hill, or tree, or on the sky,

But his sweet spirit robes them like the air.

   Kath. A loving brother and a gentle playmate.

   Iso. So firm and strong, yet full of tenderness.

   Kath. So rich in gifts and many-sided powers.

   Iso. Thinker, who follows truth where Plato led.

   Kath. Poet, within the mirror of whose eye

With double brightness shines the summer cloud.

   Iso. Musician, in whose sympathetic ear

All nature sounds its sweetest symphonies.

   Kath. True priest, whose own soul has its bread

       from God,

And fain would help his brother's hunger too.

   Iso. All this, all this, and I am far too poor,

Too mean a nature to be set with his.

It ought to be some woman richly souled

To shine with him, and to enhance his light.

I wrong him; but I cannot yield my place—

My own poor planet's dark without this sun.

Oh, yet I will be to him all I may.

Haste with me, Kate, up to the bright hill-top,

And look if anywhere there round about

We see him riding hither o'er the plain.   [*Exeunt.*

SCENE II.

The same. HAMILTON *and* ISOBEL *walking.*

Iso.· Yours was no lonely exile, then?

Ham.   No, sweet;

Fathers I found, and brothers there in spirit.

Iso. Nor profitless ?

Ham.   No, for we grow to strength

If we but hear the voice of noble men ;

And nowhere in this world have nobler met

Than now in Marburg in the land of Hesse.

I see them, friends and kind companions.

Under cool arches, over sunny flags---

Lately a nest of the Dominicans,

Where all the day they lounged, and laughed, and
     lay—

Now walks a studious band with fluttering robes,

Quick step, and faces lit with Christ's own flame,

Earnest in converse, laying thought to thought

To build God's Church up from its rot and wreck,

That once more heavenly light o'erspread the world.

From all lands have they come—East, West, North,
     South.

TYNDALE, who prints God's Word in English there :

LAMBERT, my own dear teacher, one whose faith
Rolls like the great tide of his native Rhone.
God bless you, comrades, Marburg *lebe hoch !*

   Iso. 'Mid such content why thought you to return?

   Ham. Two magnets drew me—duty, love, and
     you.

   Iso. Tell me of Luther and his Katherine.

   Ham. Theirs was a sweet home, Isobel, and sweet
To be its guest and share its happiness :
To see the doctor sit in his great chair,
Books at his elbow, and a tankard too—
His child upon his knee, to whom he told
Quaint German legends, or the history
Of God's own Jewish folk; to hear him sing
Some song of Fatherland, or hymn his own—
One sounding like the trumpet of a host
That rallied them for the Lord.   His words to me
Clove to the heart of things as with an axe.

Never in all my life have I beheld
So God-reliant, healthful, strong a man.
Katherine moved all about with word and smile
And busy fingers, perfecting the joy
Of that sweet household, that most novel place,
A churchman's home.

  Iso.   And even such as theirs
Will our home be; say, will it not, my love?

  Ham. Dear Isobel, to-morrow sees us wed,
And, God knows, if I could I'd make your life
Happier than ever woman's.

  Iso.   Oh, it will,
It must be happy.

  Ham.   Grant it, kindly heaven!
And yet almost my heart misgives, and says
I bring thee certain sorrow and not joy,
And I should bear my lot alone, not ask
That you should share it. Oh, my Isobel,

Sometimes I think that it were kindest done
To grasp thy hand but once, as I do now,
And quit it thus, and say, " Farewell for earth—
Keep we our love for heaven."

  Iso.   My Hamilton !
Oh, what means this?

  Ham.   Not little, love, but much.
I fear some lightning-stroke that scathes my branch
May strike the sweet bird sheltering there.

  Iso.   Oh, why,
Why these foreboding miserable words?

  Ham. I know not now, but much of late I feel,
Life spreads for me no shining reach of hope :
Ever at hand some trouble of darkness broods
That swallows up my years.   I cannot pierce it,
Nor look in thought beyond, and see myself
Moving upon the landscape of the world.
Earth's long enjoyment is for other men :

For me there is some task—I know not what—
To do, and then begone.

 Iso.   Oh, chase these fears;
They come in minds o'erwearied with deep thought.
Fear not for me, for, see, I have no fear;
The happiest lot I ask is to share thine.

 Ham. Will it not vex thee if a passing eye
Views me askance, to read there "heretic"?

 Iso. Nay, for I know you wise, and good, and
    true—
More than a world of ignorant and blind.
And think you not a woman loves him most
Whom men desert?   He then is most her own—
Most needs her love.   When all the herd flies off,
Still stands the hind beside her wounded mate.

 Ham. Kind heart!   Yes, I can easily believe
No scorn of man would make you scorn me too:
The world has learnt ere this how woman's faith

Can cling through ill report.   Yet there is more—
My life is perilled——

  Iso.   So a soldier's is.
His wife must anguish while the battle news
Is on the way, and yet she shares his lot.
But is there fear?

  Ham.   I cannot tell.

  Iso.   Oh, then,
Love, you shall take me to the Fatherland,
To that sweet valley you have told me of;
You said how fair it was.

  Ham.   No lovelier spot
Shines anywhere upon this earth of God.
There flows the Lahn in many a gleaming curve,
Bordered with gardens, level, trim, and square—
A maze of walks and hedgerows.   On each side,
Far up and down, run alleys poplar-lined,
Creaking with ox-wains of the peasant folk.

Round are the hills and all the rich pine-woods,
Where here and there climb little winding paths,
Red, over roots of trees zigzagging up
To nooks of vantage where you turn and look,
And lo ! the vale beneath you all aglow,
Breathing the incense of ten thousand flowers—
Linden and white acacia, vine and bean.
Pure is the air; the swifts that flash and wheel
Shriek o'er the golden scene for ecstasy.
Here crowds the ancient city, tier on tier
Of steep streets clambering upward to the Schloss,
Quaint gables, terraces, and vine-clad bowers.
Below rise Saint Elizabeth's twin spires—
Oh, sweet their silver bells at eventide ring !
But sweeter there in men's hearts ring the bells
Of faith and freedom, brotherhood and joy.

 Iso. There will we go and spend long happy days ;
And you will walk, love, with the wise good men,

While I will trim the house, and round our board
Will be sweet converse of the newer time.

Ham. My place is here in Scotland, Isobel;
But yet I hope even here peace may be found.
Methinks, in these short months since I went hence,
That light has grown and tolerance increased.
Fain would I trust that here a man may speak
As the Christ bade him, without risk or fear.

Iso. Be sure of it; the truth must win men's
hearts.

Ham. Pray God it may! I hear my sister's voice.

KATHERINE *in the distance singing.*

Is it the robin's low note I hear,
  Bidding me know the sweet summer away?
Yes, yes, I see that the leafage is sere,
  I scent the autumnal decay.

Over my heart comes a breath of the tomb,
   Sadder the light smiles, the air has a sigh.
Ah! did I dream that above me would bloom
   For ever this brightness of sky?

Soon cruel winter comes blowing so cold,
   Blighting the blossom and shedding the leaf;
Soon cruel change comes, as ever of old,
   Bringing the glad heart a grief.

Ham. Come, let us join her in the other walk.

                                     [*Exeunt.*

ACT III.

SCENE I.[1]

St Andrews; night. HAMILTON *alone, reading.*

Ham. This lamp burns low, its flickering shadows
vex
The weary sight.   My books, a while lie closed.
Now like a night-bird flies my thought abroad,
And beats its baffled wings against the stars,
And wheels about the world, and sees èarth's ball
Rounding amid the heaven.   This side is dark,
And over snow-clad roofs of sleeping streets
Our vast cathedral rears its pinnacles,

[1] See Note C, p. 112.

Louring and solemn.   Yon side is gilt with day.

Flash all the bays with waves ; o'er coral crests,

Round which the foam is sparkling, light canoes

Are leaping, and on shore the wigwams smoke.

Over the tawny soil move dusky men,

Under palm trees, 'mid trail of glowing flowers ;

And lo ! I see one kneel at a rude shrine,

Beating his breast, and lifting eyes to heaven.

All this is God's—the earth, the men, the shrines :

He holds it in the hollow of His hand.

Shall we not leave, then, each man well content

With his poor idol, since it serves his need ?

Why should we break it, and upon its head

Trample in wrath ?   But yet again we ask,

Whence comes this heat in the breast, this straitening

To set some better altar in its place—

This zeal to beat down error, and to speak
The truth we think out till men hear it of us,
That to be dumb is pain, and seems a crime?
Whence is this urging to give earth our thought
Before we die and go to God, and stand
And answer Him, " Didst speak the word I bade?"
God's is this prompting, and it serves His will.
Even as He bids the seed fly eager abroad,
To clothe His world with verdure of all kind,—
The flower for beauty, and the fruit for food,—
It flies, it springs, it swims o'er leagues of sea,
Till deserts bloom—the lonely place is glad.
The coral isle, new risen, receives its palm ;
Even so He prompts us sow His world with truth,
That thus it still may rise from stage to stage,
From creeping lichen thought to noble growth
Of knowledge of Himself and life's great laws.
Yes, yes, my God, I have a work from Thee—

A minister to men ; teacher of souls ;
Intrusted with the light that came in Christ !
I would not be that hatefullest thing on earth,
A faithless priest.

> (*Lifting a paper from the table, then seeing*
> Archbishop Beaton, *who has entered.*)
> Archbishop !

Arch. B.   Pardon me.
I startle you, but entered without noise,
Because I would not have a tattle go
That I came hither at this midnight hour.
You guess what brings me—that unpleasant paper
Which now is in your hand, and summons you
Before our court to-morrow.   Take my word,
It greatly went against my wish to send it ;
But then, you see, I had no longer option.
You have been too outspoken, and men clamour.
'Tis " Hamilton " I hear from morn to night ;

" Hamilton has been preaching here and there,

Saying most hateful and pernicious things ;

Can you permit this sort of thing go on,

Archbishop? is't your duty? "—so they speak.

They take my peace away with " Hamilton."

I come here as your friend ; you must give up

This dangerous game.

> *Ham.*   I cannot cease to speak

The truth.

> *Arch. B.* The truth ! now, who knows *that* ?

It is your way of thinking, but that man's

May be as good. We've nothing absolute.

> *Ham.* My truth is this, the best God gives my
> soul.

> *Arch. B.* Well, well, then keep it for your own
> soul's use.

But mark you, here a certain form of truth

Is in possession, old and venerable—

Delusion much of it, quite probably;

But then mankind's delusions give you basis

For institutions of much social use—

Why should you touch them?   Well, then, here, we

    stand—

The Church, I, and the rest of us—and you,

You shake that foundation, threatening all.

    Ham. I cannot hold my peace.

    Arch. B.   Best that you tried it;

For, let me say, things now grow serious.

Or say you somewhat modified your words,

Made them less harshly grating to our ears.

Why show the gulf so gaping 'twixt your thought

And the Church doctrine?

    Ham.   But it is my wish

To show my thought, not hide it.

    Arch. B.   Obstinate!

Now, let me tell you plainly how it stands,

If you obey this summons and appear—

Though possibly you're otherwise advised.

 Ham. You taunt me, but I will appear.

 Arch. B.   You will?

When you shall stand, then, in the face of our court,

Your language·must be other than 'tis now—

You must retract——

 Ham.   Never! Before your court

I will assert the truth, and give its grounds,—

Prove it from God's own page.

 Arch. B.   You are a fool!

Think you we meet to hear your argument,

And be converted—to sit still and listen

While you, forsooth, expound—be lectured to

And schooled by you? No, no; but we intend

To sweep this Luther leaven from the land

You have been spreading, and to clear this soil

From damnable invasion of Dutch error.

We have been too forbearing, but that's over.

Now will we act, and sharp, though Scotland blaze

From side to side like hell, with fires that shrivel

Heretics into charcoal !

  Ham.   I have done

My duty in God's sight—will do it still.

Threats cannot move me, all the cost is counted.

I speak as God bids to my countrymen,

To men here perishing for lack of knowledge,

Kept in gross darkness and idolatry,

Shut out from Christ's true gospel and pure word.

I speak as God has taught me all my life—

Ay, day by day in all I've thought or read,

Or known or learned—until the thing has grown

Rooted so in my heart that you may tear

My heart out, but not tear away that truth.

Archbishop, I have lain on the wide hills

And spread my soul to God ; I've watched the night,

Sleepless upon my bed, and wept my prayers ;
I've read whatever thought of wisest men
Breathes from their soul in books ; I sought for truth,
Both what a man might live by and might preach ;—
Oh, agony of inward suffering !
I loathed the current and the common things
They offered me, impossible of belief :
And yet I hoped that somewhere there was help
For my poor soul, some bread to feed its hunger
From Him who satisfies all living things ;
That under all the folly and the froth—
The untrue legends, the Mass miracles,
The cobweb systems and theologies—
Was truth that had made glad the heart of the world.
At the Christ's feet I sat and heard His words—
Heard Jesus preach on Galilean hills ;
Then did the day-star rise, and it was morn ;
I saw the light, and saw ten thousand faces

Turn on me, shining, from all lands and times,
And saw them smile—" Brother, thou too hast joined
The Church invisible."

 Arch. B.   And yet all this
May be mere error?

 Ham.   No. But be it so ;
Error I trust my God to pardon me—
Not cowardice or treachery.

 Arch. B.   Nay, now,
Your earnestness is excellent, commands
My admiration ; 'tis a quality
Suiting to youth ; age, alas ! tames us all—
·Makes us a trifle worldly, too, maybe.
Say I befriended you, as possibly
I might incline? I still am only one ;
Others there are may press things, for you see
Self-preservation is a potent force.
We can't despise you and your comrades, now

You grow to power.   Power still is on our side,
Which this self-preservation bids us use.
You said you meant t' appear before our court?
   Ham. I did.
   Arch. B.   You must do no such foolish thing;
You must withdraw yourself from this a while—
It is the way to spare us both some trouble;
You have gone hence before, do so again.
Start with the first light.   Lest you're unprepared
For such a sudden journey, here are means
To take you where you will.

                    (*Laying money on the table.*)

   Ham.   Never again!
Once have I gone—well, call it fled—but now
I stay and face the worst.
   Arch. B.   'Tis death, then.
   Ham.   Hard!
Hard! yet all men die once; some time it comes;

A few short clock-ticks more or less—what's that?

Nothing! but it is much that we keep true

In duty's orbit, suffering no mere breath

Of fear to blow us from it where we wander

In dismal outer spaces, grieving God,

While demons sneer " another soul has lost

The purpose and the glory of his life,"

To buy the respite of some coward years

With everlasting failure and contempt!

Archbishop, look where through the pane a star

Shines in a rift of heaven : yon murky cloud

Comes driving as to sweep it from night's face ;

Now the blast bellows, and the air's embroiled ;

But wait, wait—see, is it not shining still,

With age-long calm?   It is a steadfast soul

That is not harmed, let earth do all its worst,

And triumphs when the short blast over-blows.

   Arch. B. Your new-wed wife !

Ham.   Silence! That argu-
ment
You shall not use; leave my own wretched heart
To urge that home; stay not to torture me,
But hence, begone! Oh, my poor Isobel,
And my sweet babe unseen! the flesh is weak,
The flesh is weak. 'Tis nature opes her founts
And pours these tears. Now to curse God and—live:
This is the devil's whisper; down, fiend, down!

Arch. B. Might you not even yet?

Ham.   Still in this
place?
I thought you had been gone; away, away!

Arch. B. Still obstinate?

Ham.   My last word's uttered:
go!

Arch. B. Your blood on your own head, then. I
am gone.   [*Exit.*

Enter ISOBEL *from an inner apartment.*

Iso. Methought, love, I heard voices even now ;
Was no one here? I am bewildered, sure—
Such fearful dreams I had ; it seemed men came
Dragging you from me, and I shrieked and woke.

  Ham. Sweet, get thee to thy chamber and thy
     sleep,
Thy health is tender ; women take such fears
At times. 'Tis chill, I hear the falling snow
Beat on the pane. To thy warm bed again.

         (Leads her to the door of the apartment
            and shuts it.)

O God, this is too terrible ! O God,
Be near me in this grief ! my Father, strength !

                (Kneels)

SCENE II.

Airdrie—morning. RALPH *driving cows.*

Ralph. Any way but the right way, cross-grained
    brutes;
You're just like folk.

Enter HORSEMAN.

Hors.   Ho! is your master up?

Ralph. And who may you be?

Hors.   That's not to the
    point;
Say, is your master up?

Ralph.   Point or no point,
I'll know who asks.

Hors.   Blockhead! I am in haste

Ralph. You'll be in no such haste the day you're
   hanged,
Or I mistake.

Hors.   You rude, uncivil slave,
A life's at stake.

Ralph.   But not my life, maybe.

Hors. Yours! what is yours more than this fly's I
   crush
Upon my horse's neck? Young Hamilton's.

Ralph. The Lord forbid!

Hors.   Amen, and so say I.
They'll burn him, though, before the day be done,
Unless your master and his friends fetch help.
Now, will you quickly bring me where he is?

Ralph. That will I; stop but till I close this gate;
Now follow me. I think he's close at hand;
A moment since I saw him in the court.   [*Exeunt.*

DUNCAN, HORSEMAN, *and* RALPH.

Dun. You're ready mounted; ride you quickly
    round
To every house that stands upon the land.
Ride to the Melvilles too at Carnbee,
Bid them bring all their men. Say how it stands—
That our dear Hamilton is prisoner
In that infernal den 'neath Beaton's hold,—
Is to be tried to-day—a wretched farce,—
That much we fear his death's resolved upon,
Unless we save him from their tigerish claws.
Curse on the stormy night! I hear the Firth
Raging this morning murderously loud;
No boat could cross. Sir James's help is stayed
Upon the other side; all lies with us.
Said you the Archbishop had a numerous force?

Hors. They thronged St Andrews as I passed
    thereout,

And still by every road were pouring in.

All yesterday they gathered hour by hour.

    Dun. Ride, then, away!—Ralph, rouse the men
    about;

See that the horses have a double feed.

Get their shoes sharped, the roads are keen with ice.

Set the swords to the grindstone, give them edge.

If we lack numbers, we will make that up

With our arm's pith, and with our heart's hot rage.

                        [Exeunt.

SCENE III.

Outskirts of St Andrews. PRIOR CAMPBELL;
DUNCAN *following.*

Cam. I had not thought that it would have this
end.

Oh, wretched me !   [*Exit.*

Dun.   Infamous traitor, stand !

Shall a cowl shelter such a scoundrel head ?

Enter SOLDIERS, *who strike* DUNCAN'S *sword out*
of his hand.

Soldiers. Yield, yield !

Dun.   I am disarmed, no help but

yield.

Your chief's name ?

Sol.　　　　　Duncanson.

Dun.　　　　　　　To him then take me.

　　　　　　　　　　　　　[Exeunt.

SCENE IV.

St Andrews, near St Salvator's College.

WOMAN *with boy.*

Woman. Haste, haste, my child, out of this dread-
　　ful street !

Oh, the dear lad, he has a mother too,

And a young wife !　Oh, cruel, cruel world !

　Boy. Mother, they'll not do that when I'm a man ;
I will kill Beaton.

　Wom.　　　　Whist, whist, foolish boy !

Oh, let us quickly hence.　　　　　　*[Exeunt.*

Man, *running.*

Powder, more powder ;
Himself has cried for it.   [*Exit.*

Another, *do.*

More kindlings here !
This plaguy pile is hard to set alight ;
The wood is green as grass.   [*Exit.*

Baker, *with a bundle of straw under his arm.*

Here is dry straw.
Bunglers, did they light ovens every day,
More skill they'd have.   This is the fail-me-never.
Thrust it well in upon the windward side,
And give it air.   [*Exit.*

CITIZENS, *meeting.*

1st Cit.   What ails you; why so fast?

2d Cit. Stop, friend, and turn, else will your eye-
balls crack

With sudden horror.   The young Hamilton——   •

   1st Cit. Ah, I remember; 'tis his trial day.

   2d Cit. Trial and death day!   At the college gate

Even now he dies in agonies of fire.

You speak of trial; yes, this morn they tried him

After a fashion, and condemned him too;

Sent for a warrant, and with murderous haste—

Because this storm holds off his brother's help,

Who chafes with force of arms on yon side Forth—

Piled up the wood, and bound him to the stake.

I lingered, looking for some happy turn,

I knew not what, to save the final act—

Rescue, relenting pity, timely yielding—

When suddenly a flash of powder blazed,

Scorching his hand and cheek. Some one cried out

To give a sign if still his faith was firm.

He gave it, holding up the shrivelled hand.

Another blaze! I sickened then, and fled.

Within the deepest chamber of my house

I run to hide me; but this horrid sight

Is branded on my brain, as I have heard

The lightning on the flesh of him it strikes

Brands all the scene it lit, and I will see

That blackened hand up-pointing till I die.

3*d* CITIZEN, *entering.*

3*d* *Cit.* This in the name of Christ, peace and
    goodwill!

2*d* *Cit.* How goes it now?

3*d* *Cit.*   Thank God, I think
    he rests.

The pile was long of kindling, but at length
A blast blew from the sea, and then it roared
In sudden fury, flinging blasts of flame
All round about, and scorching some stood near ;
At which the people shouted, and made sport
To see them running beating with their hands
Their burning garments.   'Mid the shining flame
I saw the martyr's face.   Somewhat it sank
Upon his bosom, and it looked like peace.

   2d Cit. His soul is 'scaped, only the flesh remains.
See, see, a smoke is curdling o'er the roofs,
And spreading blackness on the face of heaven.
Oh, what a horror in that pitchy cloud !
How sickening and repugnant to the sense !
Great God ! that smoke blows hither ; let us hence.

                      [Exeunt.

SCENE V.

Outside the town—moonlight. DUNCAN, RALPH.

Dun. What haggard and distracted wretch comes
here,
Clutching his head in his hands?   Can this be
Campbell?

PRIOR CAMPBELL.

Cam. I fled thee once—see, now I run to thee.
Thou wouldst have slain me then — would 't had
been done,
I had been spared these hours of agony.
Out thy sword now, and plunge it deeply down
Into this wretched, wretched, wretched heart.
See, I am on my knees and my throat bare.
Mayhap a fount of blood will quench this fire

That burns my brain.   Waters will not—not seas.
My clothes are wet.   I rushed into the sea,
But the black wave uprose above my head
And drew back shuddering, and all ocean roared.
Ocean !   No, it was hell !   Voice upon voice
Bellowed and cried aloud upon my guilt,
To the whole world, swelling and swelling still, .
Till the whole world was filled with horrible sound ;
Then burst a great noise on me, and a hand
Smote me, and hurled me breathless on the rocks
Among the slimy sea-weed.   Out I crawled
And ran, I knew not whither, but I ran.
My brain is burning : spare me not, but kill.

   Dun. Poor frantic wretch, away! I would not harm
     thee.

   Cam. See, I will aid thee to loose out the blade,
And grasp thy fists, and help thee urge it home.

             (*Seizing the hilt of* DUNCAN'S *sword.*)

Dun. Away! hold off! else I will smite thee down.

Cam. Avenge thy friend, man — ay, thy friend
   and mine.

We read our books together, seat by seat ;

We walked entwined like lovers, while the light

Of evening faded on the western hills,

And as the aurora flashed its quivering beams,

Now pale, now rose, among the blossoming stars,

So flashed our minds throughout all realms of
   thought—

The past, the future, heaven, earth, life and death,

Blending alternate—now 'twas his, now mine,

Adventurous, hopeful. Oh, sweet days of youth !

Yet I deserted, sold him—oh, my brother !—

To fearful pangs. Let me not think of it.

Coward I was, and slave, and feared men's face.

Oh, I could pierce my eyes to hide the sight

They see for ever, if they ope or shut

By night or day.   Nothing now hear my ears
But sound of fires—nothing my memory holds
But one wild day.

                What was it that he said?
" Meet me before the judgment-bar of God
Within these days."   I am in haste to go.
I have no rest till, flung before his feet,
I cry this word, " My brother, see my sorrow ! "
Then, though he turn his sainted face away,
And at God's word fiends drag me straight to hell,
He will have heard my cry and known my sorrow—
Heard my true cry and known my bitter sorrow.
Wilt haste me hence?   No?   Yet it needeth not ;
Within this head the poor mad brain dies fast.

                            (*Falls.*)

  Dun. Help, Ralph! he falls; we must be merciful :
" Vengeance," the Lord has said, "vengeance is mine."
See how his features writhe and his lips foam !

Water, Ralph, water! fetch some from the brook;
My sword's round hilt will serve instead of cup.
I will support him meanwhile; rest his head
Upon my knee.

      Oh, great God over all,
Thine own dear Son prayed for His enemies,—
Look on this guilty, miserable wretch
In Thy compassion, which is infinite.

       (RALPH *brings water.*)
Some on the forehead, some between the lips.
In vain—he dies; no breath, no beat of heart;
The fixed eyes wince not at my finger's touch.
Gone!

 Ralph. And to burning hell.

 Dun.   Let us not judge;
'Tis God's to judge, not ours. Unhappy wretch,
Conscience, the torturer, o'erdid his office—
Racked him to death.

                              Poor, silent, lifeless form,
Lie gently down upon the moonlit grass,
Pale as thy face.   Since first thou trodst that grass,
A happy child, and ran to pluck its flowers,
And laughed beneath that moon in innocent glee,
How sad thy road, and what an ending this
To life's fair hopes !—guilt and remorseful grief,
Madness and death.

                              Go to the abbey, Ralph,
And tell his friends that here their prior lies
In need of burial.

                    When that is done,
Then, Ralph, to Airdrie, to my dearest wife,
And tell her all the sorrow of this day :
That our poor force was all too small to cope
With Beaton's thousands—we were overpowered ;
That Hamilton is now in heaven above,
Among the shining ones by God's own throne.

Tell her that I am taken prisoner,

My life spared only on the hard condition

That I leave Scotland.   Tell her I go south

To Beverley, and you will guide her thither.

And that sad widow, too, poor Isobel,

God comfort her ! for surely woman's heart

Never bore heavier load.   I gave my promise

To care for her if aught should happen him.

I'd sooner trust you than another, Ralph ;

You have more shrewdness than some men seem

    wiser ;

You have been faithful to me all my life,

And to my house.   Go, and God speed you, Ralph !

                [*Exit* RALPH.

O Hamilton, my brother, dear companion !

God take thy soul to His own sweetest rest.

Oh, if there be no heaven for such as thou,

Nor any hell for thy black murderers,

All is iniquity and rank confusion.
O Christ, he loved Thee, was Thy loyal servant.
He had no thought but to be true to Thee
And to Thy people, and to that sweet word
Thou bad'st him speak of heavenly faith and hope.

Ah, ye cathedral towers, black with the smoke
Of a most blessed martyr, if this hand
Held but a thunderbolt, would I not hurl it
In roaring ruin on your guilty heads?
Ha! in my frenzied eye I see you falling!
What's this?   A roar of people, and a fire—
That which slew Hamilton—bursting anew
O'er all your roofs!   Blaze, blaze avenging flames!
No drop of water for that sinner's hell.
Fling your red arms aloft and clutch these towers—
Drag them to ruin—tear the casements out—
Burst with hot blasts the doors.

Ha! do ye fly?

Is then your day of trembling now arrived?

Fly! gather all your gowns and fly, ye crew!—

Out of the land, over the edge of the world.

Politic priests, worldly Machiavels,

Spawn of the Pharisees, haters of light,

Slayers of God's own prophets, of the breed

Of those that sawed Isaiah, spilt the blood

Of agèd Paul upon a dungeon's floor,

Murdered the Christ Himself! See how your house

Is left unto you desolate! Oh, I am mad

With anger and with sorrow. Farewell, Scotland!

Farewell my home, the pleasant shores of Forth!

The freshening haur that blows from off the sea,

And happy hours in Airdrie, fare-ye-well!

[*Exit.*

SCENE VI.

The Cathedral; a dark passage; bell tolling.
Two MONKS *with tapers, meeting.*

1st Monk. Brother, why tolls the bell? It is no
    hour
Of usual office.

2d Monk.   Heaven and earth! I know not;
I groped where hangs the rope, and no hand
    stirs it.

1st Monk. Strange! and the tone, too, altered;
    hear, the brass
Sinks to a dreadful minor.

2d Monk.   Mother of God!
Ne'er heard I such a doomsday sound.

1st Monk.   The towers

Are reeling as their solid base would yield.

I quake for fear.

    2d Monk.   I, too.   Hush ! hark ! a voice !

    1st Monk. I bow me earthward, nor dare lift my
      eyes.

VOICE from above.

I am the Spirit of Truth.

I ring the knell

Of churches seeking not man's good alone—

Seeking their own ;

Of priests that utter in my name divine

No word of mine,—

The blind that sees not day,

The knave that hides the ray.

I ring the knell

Of all that lives not in immortal youth

Of fact and truth ;

Of power and pomp, wisdom and policy,

That trust in their own craft and put *me* by ;

Of all hypocrisy

And insincerity,

And whatsoever makes and loves a lie.

N O T E S.

———

Note A.

JOHN ANDREW DUNCAN (page 34).

John Andrew Duncan, at whose house some
scenes are laid, was laird of Airdrie in the east of
Fife, a spot within a mile of the author as he writes.
When a student at St Andrews, he had been in-
duced by youthful ardour to join the standard of
James IV. at Flodden. In the calamitous battle
which followed he was taken prisoner, but being

of gallant appearance, was indulgently treated by
Lord Surrey, who sent him into England and
allowed him to reside at liberty with relations of
his own in Yorkshire.   There he married an
English wife, a daughter of Dr Burnet of Beverley ;
and, already a Liberal and reformer, became under
his father-in-law's guidance a zealous Wickliffite.
On the conclusion of the war he returned to his
native land, living at Airdrie in friendly intercourse
with the reformers, clerical and lay, and making
his house their frequent and hospitable resort.

It was at this time, and at the particular date of
Lent 1527, that James Beaton, Archbishop of St
Andrews (instigated, as is thought, by his more
energetic and better-known nephew, then Abbot of
Arbroath, afterwards Cardinal), first took notice of
Hamilton.   He inquired into certain rumours con-
cerning him, found that he was "inflamed with

heresy, disputing, holding, and maintaining divers heresies of Martin Luther and his followers repugnant to the faith," and in consequence decerned him to be formally summoned and accused. He did not, however, abide that trial, but "passed to the schools of Germany," — his object being to inquire more thoroughly into the grounds of the faith he held, and in particular to see Luther.

Note B.

HAMILTON AT MARBURG (page 54).

Hamilton's resting-place for a time was the little picturesque German town of Marburg on the Lahn, a place then very notable to the world. Philip the Landgrave, Luther's friend, had recently ejected the

Dominican monks from their cloisters, and erected within the premises ·what was the earliest of Protestant universities. To be professor within it of the reformed doctrines he had invited a remarkable Frenchman, Francis Lambert of Avignon. To the spot flocked men from all countries, whose names are to be read in the venerable album still in the possession of the university. The book records the circumstances of the first erection of that place of learning, and contains a list of its earliest teachers and *alumni.* It is a deeply interesting muster-roll. The author has looked with emotion on many Scotch names which stand on its pages, and in particular on the entry, "Patricius Hamilton a Litgovien, Scotus, Magister Parisiensis."

He met there among others Walter Tyndale, the English translator of the Scriptures, and John Frith, who afterwards edited a little work of Hamilton's called 'Patrick's Places.' From that work, it may be mentioned, is taken the outline of Hamilton's Christian teaching which has been sketched in his address to the sailors at sea.

He remained in Marburg till the end of the university session, when he returned home. Shortly after he entered into marriage with a "noble lady," whose name, unfortunately, has not come down to us. Seeing, however, that their only daughter, born shortly after her father's death, was, as we know, called Isobel, the author has ventured— not without probability, he thinks, on his side—to give the same name to the brave woman who ventured in such circumstances to join her lot to that of the young martyr.

Note C.

HAMILTON AT ST ANDREWS—THE CLOSING
SCENES (page 71).

His return from abroad was in the month of
October 1527, and there is reason to believe that
he immediately devoted himself with earnestness
to teach the principles of the Protestant and evan-
gelical faith at St Andrews, as well as in his paternal
locality of Linlithgow.   Early in the next year a
second, and what proved a final and fatal, summons
was sent him by the Archbishop.   This time there
was no withdrawal on his part.   Friends saw what
was impending, and urged flight; even the Archbishop would, it is said, have preferred that he

took this course; but his mind was made up to a resolute stand. After a form of trial before the dignitaries of the Church, in which Prior Campbell, his early companion, was base enough to act the part of accuser, he was condemned as a heretic to be burnt at the stake. At noon of the same day the terrible sentence was carried out in front of the gate of St Salvator's College. This was on the last day of February 1528, the martyr being then no more than 24 years of age. His friend, John Andrew Duncan, made a strenuous effort to rescue him, raising a troop of horse, and riding into St Andrews at their head; but he was defeated and taken prisoner. The leader of the troop which took him being one Duncanson, an Angus gentleman, and the husband of his sister, he escaped with life on condition of forfeiting his property and retiring into exile. The traitor Campbell, according to the account of George Buchanan and others, died within a short period, conscience-stricken, and raving mad.

Katherine, Hamilton's sister, came herself near to sharing her brother's fate. She was put on trial for heresy in the year 1535, but escaped through the king's influence. The last notice we have of her is in a letter dated 1541, in which mention is made that she had been wife to "the last captain of Dunbar," and is then residing at Berwick.

From the death of Hamilton events moved rapidly forward.[1] No more than thirty years elapsed until the scene imagined by Duncan in the text actually took place,—the Cathedral of St Andrews blazed, and the gigantic fabric of the Romish Church fell into irretrievable ruin—a lesson and a warning.

[1] "The reik of Patrick Hamilton infected as many as it blew upon."

COLUMBUS

ORIGINALLY PUBLISHED IN 'BLACKWOOD'S MAGAZINE.'

COLUMBUS.

Now through two weary moons, the restless keels
Had journeyed onward to the Gates of Eve ;
Still fortune shone not, and no hopeful sign
Gladdened their toil with earnest of success.
Still Ocean hid within his circling arms
The land they sought, and on her thousand shores
Whispered unheard, unseen.

                      Each early morn
With eager watching eyes they scanned the verge
Of utmost ocean, and each weary eve
In sadness turned to meditate and mourn.

Yet oft in fancy's vision seemed to rise,

Far to the Westward, where the parting day

Lay throned in state, fair lands of emerald dyes,

Bright isles encircled by the purple sea;

Here were cool valleys spread, that sweeter shone

Than all the myrtle groves of fair Castile,

And here brave mountains reared their haughty
    front,

Flushed with the closing sunset's rosy light :

Oh then were leaping hearts and straining eyes !

Till Night her envious curtains closed around,

And the grey morn awoke, whose sober ray

O'ershone a weary waste of shoreless sea.

Thus day by day, a never-ending scroll,

The deep rolled out before them, and the sky

Stood like a burnished wall on every side :

And day by day the sailors' hearts grew sad :

Hope's twilight faded, and Despair's chill night
Darkened their breasts with rage, their brows with
    gloom;
Therefore they spake, and crowded as they spake
Around the Master, with strange longing eyes
And mingled looks of fear and fierce resolve.

    " Our homes are white by Palos' shore
        In the light of the autumn day,
      But we return, ah ! never more
        To Palos by the bay.
    Our bones shall roll in the restless sea,
    And matted weeds our shrouds shall be !

    " Now twice the moon has waxed and waned
      Above our head to Westward sailing,
    For land our eager eyes are strained,
      Oh labour unavailing !

Our hope is fled, and our golden dream
Passed like a mist in morning's beam.

" Tell us, shall we sail with thee
    Into the sunset's burning eye,
  Across the never-ending sea
    Still onward, till we die?
A weary sea with never a shore,
That rolls behind and spreads before,
Rides by the keel for evermore.

" On to our ruin we rush open-eyed;
  Ha! to receive us the sea-grave is wide;
  Dark grows the maddening thought!
  Home let us hie!
  Rush not on destiny!
  Tempt not the sky!
  Loved ones are calling!

They chide our delay!
Sons of the ocean
To Eastward away!—
Tarry not, brothers,
Be manful of mind;
Spread our sea-pinions
Abroad to the wind,
To Spain of our love,
To our homes by the bay;
Tarry not, brothers!
To Eastward away!"

From words to acts, to rope and helm they sprang
Like hounds unleashed; but as the huntsman's voice
Recalls the erring curs, with drooping heads
And eyes that beg for mercy to his heel,
So in the fire-glance of the Master's eye
Stayed they their mid career, and cowered abashed.

Like some old alchemist, whose toilsome years
Had stamped endurance on his iron brow,
Within whose breast, high-hoping, thwarted oft,
Had calmed to patient trust, resolved he stood,
A grand grey-headed man.

       " My men," he said,
" To this emprise I gave my youthful years,
My nights of study and my days of toil,
Poor, save in hope, until the burning thought
I moulded on the anvil of my brain
Has cooled to iron purpose : shall I now
Fail in the trial, like a faithless brand
That sells its lord ?   No, by yon Heaven I serve !
The cost is counted, and I bide my time
Through thousand troubles hopeful.   All my course
A voice has whispered ever in my ear,
' Go on, go on, Columbus ! it is thine
To plant new jewels in the ancient crowns

That rule in Europe, and to lift the Cross
For healing of another Christendom.
Go on, and prosper!' Shall I fear to press
Where points the guiding finger of my fate?
Or, having come on this our mighty quest,
So nigh success, say, shall we turn us now,
To be the jest and by-word of the time?
I cannot think ye cowards! ye are men
Dauntless of heart and resolute of will
To win regard of Heaven, and carve your names
Enduring through the ages.

                     Hear me more :
I, by my science and by signs, do know
That one short day our enterprise shall crown,
And fortune's cup brim o'er.

                     Mark well my words :
But once yon sun shall lip the Western wave
Ere this fair land, which night and day I've sought

As one that searches for a long-lost love,
Shall rise from ocean like a smiling bride,
And toil be glorious gain."

      Slowly they passed,
As clouds when skies are wrathful, heavy-browed,
And big with silent thunder, till soft sleep
Upon her dreamy bosom laid each head,
And kissed each weary eyelid into rest,
That not the angry sea that groaned around,
And smote the ship with weary buffetings,
Could break; but still the memory of their woes
Waked, and with cruel fancies shook their souls.
One wept in sleep, and one did clap his hands
And murmur "Land!" Anon he shrieked aloud,
"'Tis false, I tell ye—false, and we are lost!
The sea takes all." Sadly the Master heard,
And his big heart was bowed with many griefs.
He knelt him lowly on the midnight deck,

And his strong wish went heavenward, while the
   ship
Drove onward through the darkness of the night.

Again the dawn, again the king-eyed sun
Reigned in the welkin, and the day was full;
Again on either side the waters rode
And sparkled to the noon.   But on the tide
Came sailing slowly flowers and golden fruits,
New launched from land, and birds whose procreant
     nest
Ne'er lay on barren cliff or sea-beat rock,
But in the leafy covert of the woods
Securely hung; bright birds, of rainbow dyes,
Flashing their gleaming pinions in the sun,
Made sweetest music round the airy mast.
Auspicious signs! and all their hearts were glad.
And while the day still lingered on his flight,

And evening's eyes were peering in the East,
Fronting the solemn skies on deck they stood,
Their heads uncovered all for reverence;
With souls attuned with gratitude they sang,
And their big voices shook with o'er-fraught joy:—

   " Mother of pity and fountain of love!
    Who in yon azure sky reignest above,
      Hope of the mariner! Queen ever fair!
    Look on our lowliness!
      List to our prayer!

   " In gladness our joy, and in sorrow our stay,
    To whom but to thee may the mariner pray?
      Now by thy Holy One's passion and shame,
    Adoring, imploring,
      We call on thy name.

" From lightning, and tempest, and path-hiding cloud,
From dangers that wait when the breakers are loud,
From powers of the air, and from powers of the
wave,
Salve Regina !
Hear us, and save !

" Send forth the breeze blowing softly beside us,
Light up the pilot-stars nightly to guide us,
Till furled are our sails in thy haven of peace,
Where hushed is complaining,
And wanderings cease ! "

A night of stars ; a night of holy calm,
For musing meet and inward communing.
The fiery day-flood through the vast had rolled,
The glory and the hum, and left it now

A temple set for prayer, solemn and wide,
Wherein ten thousand living tapers shone—
Shrine of the universe, the house of God
Made not with hands. And all the deep lay still,
And looked in wonder on the shadowy blue :
Softly the night-winds sighed, and, stooping low,
Whispered strange secrets in the ocean's ear—
A night so still, as though mute nature saw
The dawning chance, and hushed in reverent awe.

Praise now the Lord, O Master, with thy soul !
And all thy heart be gladness for His love !
For all thy sorrow, here is sweetest joy ;
For all thy labour, here is full remeed ;
Be now the courtly scorn, the slander vile,
The weary wandering, the hope delayed,
All, all forgot that erst did thee annoy :
Take now thy fill of ease, be large in joy.

Lo! in the West a pale unsteady light
Shines in the mirk, and darts its silver rays—
A trembling gleam, now here, now passed away
Behind the shadowy curtains of the night,
Mocking the ken.   Oh happy, blissful beam!
Bearer of joy to sorrow-laden souls,
Sweeter than word of comforting that falls,
Like softest music in a stricken ear;   .
Welcome as ever pilot-lamp that guides
The sea-tossed sailor home, shine out, fair ray!
Kindle Hope's dying torch to ecstasy.
It beacons *thee*, Columbus; it is set,
A guiding lamp upon the New World's front,
To light thee to her shores; a taper fair
Within thy lady's casement burning bright,
Telling of welcome glad.

                But if it shine
In monarch's lofty dome or peasant's cot—

Whether it gleam o'er cities many-towered,
Or o'er the desert wild keep lonely watch—
Whether it shine o'er lands of weal or woe,
Contented rest, the daylight all shall show.

Distant and dim against the mellow sky
Loomed the new land, and on her dusky brow
The mist of morning lay.   Hueless her form,
As mid-day shadows on a sunlit wall;
For yet the day was not, but round the verge
Glimpses of glory from the under sky
Girdled the ocean with an amber zone,
And broader grew the dawn.   Star after star,
Quenching her tiny lamp in the grey sky,
Fled heavenward, and the deserted moon
Hung like a faded lily in the west.
Upward and onward, spreading warily,
Blushed the new morn, till from the glowing east,

Ruddy and glorious as the golden gates
That open on eternal summerland,
Outleapt a living ray of saffron sun,
Tripping to westward on in silent mirth,
Waking the beauty of the slumb'ring earth,
Till the wide vault o'erhead in sunshine bloomed,
And all the sea laughed upward to the sky.

Fair lay the land ; all green and dewy-fresh,
As if but yesterday the morning stars
Had o'er its birth their hallelujahs sung,
Creation's latest labour, and her best.

A lovely land ; of hills and shady vales,
And streams that by the roots of leafy trees
Stole seaward ever with a silver chime.
Far up the slope a sea of wavy boughs
Shook merrily, from off their leafy locks

Tossing the dewdrops to the sun.

　　　　　　　　　　　　 Beneath

The mossy sward that clasped the gnarled stems

Crept downward to a verge of sunny sands,

Besprent with random flakes of creamy spray.

All round the beach the ripple laughing ran,

And by each jutting peak the sunlit wave

Leapt on the rocks and clapped its briny hands ;

Shouted and rose, and shouted evermore

To see the strangers come.   While the low wind,

Heavy with breath of flowers and spiceries,

Balmy as summer breezes of Seville,

Lifted the lazy canvas languidly.

The greenwood's thousand singers winged around,

Filling the air with tuneful welcomings ;

And, sight most strange, from out the leafy shades

Came mild eyed men, like sylvan deities,

Unclothed, with tawny brows, and gazed on them.

This was the land, and grief was turned to joy;
This was the land, and all their toil was o'er;
This was the land, and where the Master stood
They turned in transport of delirious joy,
And laughed, and sobbed, and kneeling clasped his
  knees.

THE END.

PRINTED BY WILLIAM BLACKWOOD AND SONS.